EXPLAINING
Grace and Salvation
Generous, Undeserved, Co-operation

EXPLAINING
Grace and Salvation
Generous, Undeserved, Co-operation

DAVID PAWSON

ANCHOR RECORDINGS

Copyright © 2019 David Pawson

The right of David Pawson to be identified as author of this Work has been asserted by him in accordance with the Copyright, Designs and Patents Act 1988.

First published in Great Britain in 2019 by
Anchor Recordings Ltd
Synegis House, 21 Crockhamwell Road,
Woodley, Reading RG5 3LE

No part of this publication may be reproduced or transmitted in any form or by any means, electronic or mechanical, including photocopy, recording or any information storage and retrieval system, without prior permission in writing from the publisher.

**For more of David Pawson's teaching,
including DVDs and CDs, go to
www.davidpawson.com**

**FOR FREE DOWNLOADS
www.davidpawson.org**

**For further information, email
info@davidpawsonministry.org**

ISBN 978-1-911173-99-1

Printed by Ingram Spark

This booklet is based on a talk. Originating as it does from the spoken word, its style will be found by many readers to be somewhat different from my usual written style. It is hoped that this will not detract from the substance of the biblical teaching found here.

As always, I ask the reader to compare everything I say or write with what is written in the Bible and, if at any point a conflict is found, always to rely upon the clear teaching of scripture.

David Pawson

1

We have a very simple subject – grace. And it is every preacher or teacher's duty not only to tell you what is the true meaning of the Bible but what is the wrong meaning of it as well. We have this double duty to spread the truth and to warn against error. I am going to deal with three understandings of the word "grace", one of which is I believe the biblical one and two which are very common all over the world today and are not the truth, and we need to be on our guard against deception.

You will realise that I am thinking primarily of a verse or two in Ephesians chapter 2 where we are told: "it is by grace you have been saved, through faith, and this not from yourselves, it is the gift of God; not by works so that no-one can boast. For we are God's workmanship, created in Christ Jesus to *do* good works which God prepared in advance for us to do."

If you were in the northeast of England where I was brought up and you said "I'm saved by grace", they would immediately say to you: "You can't be that old." Because they would immediately think of a lady called Grace who was a great heroine in the Victorian era. Her surname was Darling, so she was known as Grace Darling. Her father was the lighthouse keeper on the outer Farne Island off the coast of Northumberland. One terrible, stormy night a paddle steamer from Edinburgh was wrecked on the rocks of the

Farne Islands and many of the people were lost, but some of them were left clinging to a rock in the middle of the ocean, and Grace spotted them from the lighthouse. If you ever go to the Farne Islands, we are talking about the outer lighthouse – the red and white one – and she persuaded her father to get a rowing boat, and they rowed out and saved the few people on the rock – in spite of the rocks and the pounding waves. I have read her biography, *Grace Darling, Victorian Heroine*. My wife and I visited the headquarters of the Royal National Lifeboat Institution (RNLI) and sure enough they had a great painting of Grace Darling on display. reminding us of what inspired our RNLI.

I introduce our subject in that way simply to show that the word "grace" is used in an incredibly different number of ways. And "Grace" has become a girl's Christian name.

There is a famous Greek sculpture of three graceful ladies which is called "The Three Graces".

We use the word "grace" in all kinds of ways. For example, we use it of graceful movement, as in ballet. Probably the most common use of it in our language today is referring to graceful movement, style, elegance or charm. We talk about someone's redeeming grace, meaning one of the best features in their character. We use it for courtesy. For example: he had the grace to apologise for what he had said or done wrong. We talk about grace as acting willingly, doing something by good grace; or being reluctant to do something – we call that bad grace. Then we use it when we are given a time to deal with payment – you can have so many days' grace before you meet this bill.

In religious usage, we use it as a title for bishops. I remember the story of a vicar who told his family: "Now when the bishop comes to lunch on Sunday, remember if you talk to him always to say Your Grace first." His little girl, as soon as the bishop appeared, said, "For what we are about to receive, may the Lord make us truly thankful" – because we use the word "grace" for a brief prayer of thanksgiving before a meal. Your grace is not just a title of bishops. William and Kate now have the title of Grace; as Duke and Duchess of Cambridge we must call them "Your Grace".

So the word is being used in so many different ways, but in fact, because we are now a secular, semi-pagan society, the word "grace" is dropping out of use, because originally it is a religious word, a Christian word; and since we are no longer a Christian nation, it is not a word that springs readily to our lips. It is probably older people who use it more than young people today. I have never heard a young person use this word. Yet, to Christians, it is one of the most precious words in the whole language. It is used only twenty times in the New Testament, and that is not very often. Some other words, like "love", are used many times, but grace is quite a rare word and it is usually applied to God. All three persons in the godhead are given the title of grace in our New Testament. God the Father, the grace of God; the Lord Jesus – the grace of our Lord Jesus Christ. The Holy Spirit is given the same title – the Spirit of grace – in Hebrews chapter 10. Most of those occasions are about the Lord Jesus Christ. He is the supreme example of grace in the New Testament.

Interestingly enough, the man who uses it more than anybody else is Paul. His background was more an example of grace than anybody else in the New Testament so he naturally uses the word more than others. This was a man who had been imprisoning and persecuting Christians and trying to destroy the church. The Lord Jesus appeared to him and made him the greatest missionary there ever was – that is grace. Paul was very conscious of that; and when he spoke about his old life, he was virtually saying: there but for the grace of God went I. So it is not a common word in the scripture. It is applied to God. When it is applied to people, it means gratitude and the word for it in Greek is "charis", from which we get out words "charity" and "charismatic", and a whole lot of other words. But when it is applied to human beings, it means that they are thankful. In fact the Greek word for "I thank you" is "eucharisto". So if someone passed you food at the table, you would say "eucharisto". That is why the Lord's Supper is called in some churches the Eucharist. You may have wondered why. It is not just a high church term for the breaking of bread, it means that when you come and take the bread and the wine, you are saying one big thank you for the grace of Jesus, the grace of Father, Son and Holy Spirit.

Now let me shock you. There is no such thing as grace. Do you know why? Because it doesn't exist by itself. There is no such *thing* as grace. You cannot say grace is a kind of package that you can pack up and give to people. No, grace is always found in persons. There are gracious people, gracious persons, but there is no such thing as grace. That is why we need to remember that grace is an attribute of a person, always: it doesn't exist by itself. That is one of the fundamental mistakes people make. When they sing the hymn *Amazing Grace* they seem to be thinking of a *thing* called grace, but there is no such thing. You cannot say the word "grace" without thinking of the person in whom that grace resides. Yet, even so, in scripture the noun is used but no adjectives. You do not find the word "gracious" in scripture, only the word "grace", and every time you find it, it is pointing to a person. It is not only an attribute of that person, it is an action of that person; it is something they *do,* not just something they are. It is the grace of God, the grace of our Lord Jesus Christ. We would not be here but for grace, but it is a person who was full of grace for us. So it is the definition of the word "grace" that is going to occupy us.

So what do we mean by "grace"? Well, let me tease

out the flavour of it. The first flavour of the word "grace" is *generosity*. It means to give, and to give on a lavish scale. When we say "grace" it means that God is generous, extremely generous, lavishly generous. He has *poured out* his grace upon us. That is the first major thing: it is to give something. Indeed, the Queen uses the word "grace" for some of her residences that she doesn't need, which she gives, rent free, to her relatives and friends – and they are called "grace and favour" residences.

It is to give something free of charge; it is sheer generosity, and grace is characteristic of givers. Even when it is applied to human beings, it also implies that people are so grateful for what they have received from the Lord that they are generous to others in turn. The grace flows through them and they are also good givers. It is a mark of having been touched by the grace of the Lord that you are a good giver, that you are generous, and that you have got his reckless giving. Someone asked why the devil should have all the world's best givers. And so, Christians become known for their generosity. They have received grace and that somehow stimulates in them a desire to be generous as well. So that is the first flavour of grace: to be very generous, to give and to give again, and to give in an unlimited way.

The second flavour of the word is that grace is not only generous, it is *undeserved*. It is to give to the undeserving, to those who not only have done nothing to deserve it, but have done many things *not* to deserve it. It is to give to people who may not be grateful. I remember a Methodist deaconess working in the east end of London. Somebody said to her: "With all the good things you are doing for people, you really must be getting an awful lot of gratitude from them.

She replied, "Don't you believe it. They just grumble."

"Then why do you go on giving to them?"

Of course her answer was, "Grace." Because grace gives

to the undeserving, to those who are not grateful, to those who have done wrong things to you. It is to do something for your enemy, to those who don't like you, to those who rebel against you. And that is the grace of God – that he offers his grace to people who have never done anything to deserve it, and who have done many things *not* to deserve it. So that is another meaning of the word "grace" which makes it an amazing word – an amazing concept. It is *generosity* to the *undeserving*.

The third flavour of the word I can only sum up in the word *initiative*. It means to take the first step; not to respond to something, but to take the first step to do something about it. It has an initiative in it. God loved us before we loved him. God called us before we called on him. It is that initiative which is summed up in the word "grace".

If you put those three words together – *generosity* to the *undeserving*, taking the *initiative*, you have got something of the flavour of this lovely word. No wonder we sing about it, and it all applies to God the Father, God the Son and God the Holy Spirit.

Now I want to say that we are all guilty of trying to improve on the Word of God by adding adjectives to his nouns. Do you know what I mean? *Amazing* grace – where did you find that word? You didn't find it in scripture. The Bible doesn't talk about amazing grace. Mind you, the person who wrote that song was a perfect example of grace. He had been a slave trader, shipping Africans from Africa to the West Indies and selling them – those who survived the horrible journey. Yet the Lord met that man, changed him, turned him into a vicar. That is a miracle. So he wrote: *amazing grace, how sweet the sound....*" That is a fairly harmless adjective. I don't think it should be used because it's trying to improve on the Word of God, and the Word of God never uses an adjective. The word "grace" by itself is enough for the Bible. It has got it all in it. I say it is comparatively harmless but a lot of other adjectives that have been added to the noun in Christian circles have done damage to the word "grace". We are going to be looking at some of these later. For example, we are going to look at the word *sovereign* grace. I am sure you have heard preachers use that. You may even have sung a few hymns with that phrase in, but the Bible never uses that adjective, and it misleads us. Then, surprisingly enough, I am going to tell you that the word *free* should not be applied to grace. Yes, it is free from one point of view but from another it is not. So *free grace* is another example of adding an adjective to God's single noun which distorts our understanding. I haven't finished yet. Have you heard of *common grace*? Or *prevenient grace*? I could go on; adjectives have been poured by human beings into this word and I think, misled us, as we will see.

But I am concerned with one adjective that I am prepared to use against grace, and that is *saving* grace. I take that from Ephesians 2 – "by grace we are saved".

So let me begin this part of our study by asking: what does *saved* mean? Because I find that many Christians don't understand that word either. And you won't understand *saving grace* until you understand what *saving* means. It doesn't mean to be saved from hell. Jesus didn't come to save us from hell – that is a bonus thrown in. We know why Jesus came because his parents were told to call him Jesus because "he will save his people from their sins" – all of them. In other words, I want you to grasp the New Testament understanding of what it means to be saved. It means to be perfect. It means to have no trace of sin in you. It means to be restored to the image of God. It means to be made the person that God meant you to be when he made you. All that is in the word *saved*. But I am afraid cheap evangelism has made it into a fire insurance – "If you die tonight, will you go to heaven or hell? Say this little prayer after me, and I guarantee that you will go to heaven and not to hell." That is a terrible caricature of salvation; it is not the New Testament teaching.

Jesus came to save us from *all our sins*, the whole lot. That is why he died. I will explain that more fully later, but that is my understanding of "by grace we have been *saved*". Interestingly enough, the verb *save* in the New Testament occurs in three tenses. You must have heard this from some preacher. You *have been saved*, you *are being saved*, and you *will be saved*. Which means, quite frankly, no-one can be saved in a minute. It is a process that can take a lifetime – and then some. Not until you and I are perfect can we really say we have been saved. Because salvation is a process covering three different stages. The stage we call *justification* is when Jesus sets us free from the penalty of sin. The second stage of *sanctification* is when he sets us free from the practicality of sin; and the third stage, which we call *glorification*, is when he sets us free from the possibility of sin. I am looking forward to being saved. Are you? Now, don't quote me on this but I am not saved yet, as my wife would tell you. In fact, one of the things I teach that she finds very hard to accept is that one day her husband will be perfect. Now I don't know why she finds that so hard to believe. I have got to believe it about her, that one day my wife will be perfect, but I think I find that a bit easier to believe than she does the other way round. Nevertheless, one day I am going to shout for the whole universe to hear: "Once saved, always saved." That will be the day when I am totally free of sin, and even from the possibility of it. To live in a place where there is no such thing as temptation – that is salvation.

Why have I emphasised this? Because most people never seem to ask why God saves us. The answer is: he is fed up with this world. He has written it off, and it is going to finish. It has been too corrupted and polluted, not just by human selfishness, but even angelic selfishness. And even nature is not as God made it. And he is going to make a new universe. Only Christians know that. We are the only ones in the universe who believe that we are not stuck with this old world until the end; that there is going to be a brand new universe: new space, new planet earth – perfect place. For that, God will need perfect people. If you went into that new universe as you are now, you would ruin it. Do you realise that? You would spoil it for yourself, for other people and, above all, for God himself. You would pollute it.

So God has found a way of taking people like us who have ruined this world, and making us fit to live in a new one. That is what salvation is all about: making people perfect, making them good enough to go and live in a brand new universe without spoiling it for anyone. Isn't that a big plan? That is a big view of salvation. It is not just: here's your ticket to heaven, you don't need to go to hell now. That's not it. It is God saying: I have found a way of preparing you for a perfect universe so that you won't spoil it.

That is what we call salvation. It begins when we are justified by faith, it goes on when we are sanctified by the power of the Holy Spirit, and it is completed when we are glorified and made ready for that new universe. Anything less than that is not New Testament salvation. That is why Paul, for example, says in his letter to the Romans: "we are *nearer* our salvation than when we first believed." Do you believe that? You are nearer to your salvation than when you first believed. Some people say, "I was saved twenty years ago." You weren't; but you are getting *nearer* to your salvation. And I look forward to being saved – which means no more David Pawson, just the image of God in me. Isn't it great that God should think up such an amazing plan to change human beings? That is why just saying "the sinner's prayer" may be a good beginning, but it is not the end of salvation by any means.

So I tend not to use the word *saved* in the past tense because I want people to realise I'm looking *forward* to being saved. And it will all be by grace, by that generous, undeserved gift of God. So that is the first thing I want to make quite clear about what *saved* means. It means to be totally free from the sins that have made you spoil this world – for yourself, others and God. God is able to complete that salvation. He has begun a good work in us but whenever you look in the mirror, say: "God hasn't finished with me yet." He hasn't. And he *can* do it. We shall see later that he has never promised that he *will* do it; he has only told us that he is *able to*. As we shall see, that involves *keeping on believing in him*, trusting and obeying him. Because that is absolutely necessary to the second and third stages of being saved.

That is what I mean by *saving grace*. So we cannot look back and specify a point where we were saved; what we can do is to identify a point where we *began* to be saved. I began to be saved at the age of seventeen and I can look back to that, but I never say I was saved then. I always say, I began to be, and God hasn't finished with me yet. And he is *able* to complete the work he has begun. Whether he actually does will depend on me – but he is able to. I cannot do it myself; nobody can save themselves. So the question is: what are we saved from? The answer is *all our sins*, every one of them. Notice that his name means that he will save his people from their *sins* – plural; not just from sin but from their sins, all of them; and he is able to do that. That is what he came to do.

The next question is: when are we saved? The answer is *when we are perfect*, when God has finished the work he has begun, when we are ready to go into that new universe. I keep emphasising that because it is the goal of salvation. That is the whole point of being saved – that we might be fit to enter into that new world that he is going to make.

I don't know if that is new to you but I do believe it is biblical, and that is why the Bible looks to that future salvation. Peter does in his letter – talking about the salvation "ready to be revealed in the last time". Hebrews talks the same way – "Jesus will appear a second time not to deal with sin but to bring salvation to those who are waiting for him." Did you ever notice that verse? Salvation is coming to those who are waiting for Jesus' return. Why? Because "when we see him, we shall be like him for we shall see him as he is". That is the point at which I see in the New Testament I shall be fit for the new world that his Father is going to make for us.

Well now, all that is salvation. When the word "grace" (*charis* is the Greek word) is applied to you and me, it means gratitude, sheer thankfulness. What do you think is the worst sin that you can commit? Well, there is a good case in the New Testament for saying *ingratitude* is the most serious sin. Romans 1 teaches us that people don't thank God for what he has done. Because he has done things for everyone. He sends his sun and rain on the just and the unjust, the good and the evil. But that is his goodness. I don't call that his grace because the New Testament doesn't. It is what some people mean by "common grace" – that everybody experiences his goodness. That is true, but the word "grace" is reserved for those who begin to be saved and go on receiving his saving grace until one day he has saved them completely. Now that, I hope, has laid a foundation for what we want to say because the big question now is: who does the saving and how does saving happen?

I have told you already that saving is in three stages or phases. That is *how* we are saved. I would assume that most readers are in the middle phase. You have been saved from the penalty of sin, and now you are *being saved* from the practicality of sinning. It is what the old hymn "Rock of Ages" said: "Be of sin the double cure, cleanse me from its guilt *and* power." At the moment, you are in that middle room being saved from the *power* of sin. But that is not the final room yet. I want to change that hymn to "be of sin the triple cure" and complete it by making sin an impossibility for me so I can live in a world where there is no temptation, a perfect world and a perfect me in it.

That is the gospel – the good news. When I preach in prison, I love to tell them that this is the gospel – that God can make you perfect. Now only God could do that because man admits no-one is perfect. There was one Man who was. There is human doubt about whether anybody could ever be perfect, but our gospel says you can be, you can start now, and when God is finished with you, you will be. That is good news and you can tell it to people in prison who are there for drug dealing and murder, and tell them they can be new people.

Years ago, I was invited to preach at a unique service in a very old church building in the Strand in London called The Temple which is surrounded by lawyers' Inns of Court, and it was the annual service for lawyers. It is a strange church. Because it is circular, the acoustics are dreadful and the pulpit is like a dock in a court. I climbed up into that pulpit, looked down and saw all these judges, headed up by Lord Denning who read the lesson, and I began the sermon by saying, "I hear the agnostics in this church are terrible." Nobody smiled, and I thought: help, we've got off on the wrong foot! It was only afterwards at a reception that someone said that was Lord Denning's favourite joke. So that fell flat. But then I gave out my text, and it was from Romans 8, "What the law could not do, God did". I said, "Now what can the law not do? Well, it can't make a bad man good. It can deter him, it can punish him, but it can't change him into a good man, much less a perfect man. But what the law could not do, God did! By sending his Son, Jesus Christ.

I don't know that it changed anything in those lawyers but I enjoyed telling them that there were things that they couldn't do that God could. And I have seen that. I cannot help but think of a Greek man called Chris Lambrianou. You may have heard of him. He was a member of the Kray Brothers gang in east London that terrorised small shopkeepers and exploited them. Chris Lambrianou, as a member of the gang, got rid of the bodies that were killed. He was therefore sentenced to fifteen years in prison, and many of those years in solitary confinement – in a cell by himself with an iron bedstead cemented to the floor, nothing in it that he could use to kill himself, though he was suicidal. He thought: if only I had some means of killing myself. But he hadn't. Then someone pushed a box of books into his cell for him to read, and on the top was a Bible. He picked it up and thought: I've heard this does you good – I'll try it. He put it under his pillow and slept on it and, for the first time, he was sleeping through the night. He thought: this Bible really does you good, so I'll wear it inside my shirt. He put it inside his shirt and he felt better and better and he thought this was really good. Then he began to read it, and then one night he woke up in the middle of the night and saw three bearded men standing at the foot of his iron bedstead. He said: "I know who you are, you're the Father, you're the Son, you're the Holy Spirit. The middle one said, "Follow me"; and Chris Lambrianou did just that. And he became a gentle man. He went on to spend his days in Oxford Court saving young men from going the way he did. The judge then sentenced young offenders: "I sentence you to spend a year with Mr. Lambrianou." Totally changed! That is the business God is in – of making bad people into good people, and good people into perfect people. And that is salvation.

What a joy it is to tell people that they can be perfect, and that God wants them to be, and that they need to be if they are ever going to be allowed into the new world. That is really where I finish this understanding of salvation. Who will God allow into a new heaven and a new earth? Only those who are totally saved from sins, and then they won't spoil it.

That is the right truth about *saving grace*. I could write a lot more on that, but that is the real meaning of grace and it leaves us with this question: who does the saving? That introduces us to one of the first errors.

There are three completely different answers in Christian circles today. They are not complementary; they contradict each other. To put it as simply as I can, the first answer says that God does the saving and we have no part in it. He does it all. That is *sovereign grace*.

Then there is a second answer: that *we* do it all. That answer fastens on texts like Acts 2 where Peter says, "save yourselves from this evil generation". That is picked out and people say: "Well there it is, it's up to you to save yourself. You know what you ought to do, then do it."

There is a middle answer: that salvation is the result of *co-operation* between God and people.

To introduce you to these three different answers which, as I say, are to be found in Christian circles all over the world, I want to put it into a picture. We seem able to see pictures more easily than just words. Imagine that we are on a beach and there is a lifeguard on a raised chair watching people swimming in the waves, for their safety. I want you to imagine that two men have got into a very strong current that is pulling them out to sea. Now then, what is going to happen? The three possibilities I want to present to you very simply are these. One is that the lifeguard waits until the two have drowned, and he says, I'm waiting because if I don't wait until they have drowned, they will probably drown me. They will struggle and drag me down too, so I'll wait until they are totally helpless and then I will go in. He waits until they have drowned and their bodies are floating, then he dives in and pulls one of them back to shore and pulls him up onto the beach and gives him the kiss of life and pumps his lungs, and the casualty coughs up sea water and comes back to life, as it were. And there it is. And you ask the lifeguard: "But what about the other man? Why did you save this one and not the other?"

He replies: "That's none of your business; I've got my reasons but I'm not telling you. Now that is one answer. I am going to be very rude and call it the Calvinist answer.

At the opposite extreme is the answer of a British monk called Pelagius; and Pelagius went as a monk to Rome on a pilgrimage and he was shocked by the immorality in the church there. He said that the real problem is that they don't make any effort to be holy. In fact, from that, he developed the idea that Christianity is a matter of making an effort and it all depends on *our* will to be a Christian and to live a Christian life. From beginning to the end, he said, it is a matter of the human will, and if people are not determined enough and not strong enough to say *I will* be a Christian, I will live the Christian life, then you end up with such poor specimens of Christianity. It was in reaction to Pelagius that Augustine, bishop of Hippo in North Africa, reacted against this over-emphasis on human will in this opposite direction. Go back to our picture. The lifeguard doesn't leave his seat now. He shouts to the two who are being swept out by the tide: "Pull for the shore, come on, you can do it. Pull hard, swim harder, come on" – and all he does is tell the two poor people in the tidal race that they are not making enough effort. Have you got that picture?

Now, in between, there is another picture: the lifeguard grabs two lifebelts to which are attached ropes and he runs down the beach and throws the two lifebelts far out to near the two who are being swept out, and he says: "Grab this and I'll pull you to shore." And of the two who are being in danger of drowning, one of them grabs the lifebelt and is pulled in, and one of them doesn't and is swept out to his death.

Now those are three pictures of three very different "theologies". Theology is the way you think about God.

One view is that God says you can't do a thing for yourself; he has to do it all. You are "dead" – you can't respond if he talks to you or throws a lifebelt to you. You can do nothing. But then you raise the question: why are some saved and some not? Who is at fault in that situation? Who is to blame? You know that many are not saved, but thank God many are. Who decides that? In the first picture, the lifeguard decided who to save and who not. In the extreme other picture – incidentally, both were lost with that one because neither of them could swim against the tide. But in the middle picture, the man who grabbed the lifebelt is saved and the man who didn't is lost. Do you follow me? I'm trying to put it as simply as I can.

Now that first picture is a picture of sovereign grace. It means that God alone decides who shall be saved, and who will not be. I think that is a terrible picture of God. It means he doesn't love everybody, and if you ask why God saves some and not others, the answer is given to you: that is the inscrutable will of God. In other words, God's not telling, and so we don't know. It is simply he has decided to save this one and not that one. That is not the God of our Lord Jesus Christ. It is not the God of my Bible. It is a god who only loves some people. My Bible says it is the will of God that all men should be saved. Which means, quite simply, that he is not to blame for those who are not. It is a very important point I am making, because the view that he decides who gets saved and who is not means that from our point of view it is a lottery. And to say that those he does save he hasn't decided because they are different from anybody else, makes it a lottery – a purely arbitrary choice as if God took the telephone directory and said, I'll save him, I won't save him. That is not the God who sent Jesus Christ, who loved the world and wanted everybody to be saved. So the answer of the middle picture I gave you is, the one who grabs the lifebelt is saved and the one who doesn't is not. That is simple; that is easy to understand.

It is to believe that God has thrown us a lifebelt called "salvation"; he wants to save us, but that we need to do something in order to take advantage of his offer. It means that grace is not *sovereign*. It is offered to us as a gift but it needs to be received. A gift needs to be appropriated. I was once trying to bring this across to a congregation somewhere near Cambridge and I had a big bar of chocolate which I put on the edge of the pulpit. I said, "That chocolate is for the first boy or girl who comes out and takes it." From then on, the eyes of every child in the congregation were fixed on this bar of chocolate. They did not listen to me at all from then on. Finally, one cheeky little boy ran up the aisle, grabbed the chocolate bar and tore the paper off. He was chewing it before he got back to his seat. And all the other children were angry with him. But he deserved it, not because he was better than anyone else, but because he took it. I offered it; he took it, and he got the benefit of it. That is my understanding of salvation. God offers it to everybody. He wants everybody to grab the lifebelt and he will pull them to the shore. But if they won't grab it… and usually the reason for not grabbing a lifebelt is that you think that you can make it on your own.

This is not salvation by works because a man who is drowning and is saved by being thrown a lifebelt and pulled to the shore, will never say he saved himself. He will always say: the one who has thrown me the lifebelt saved me. He would not dream of claiming that it was due to him that he got saved. Back to Grace Darling. Nobody ever said the people on the rock saved themselves by climbing into her boat. They all said: "She saved me; Grace saved me." And that is the way we feel about it.

But we are touching a very fundamental issue in the whole of Christian thinking. Does God do it all without our co-operation; without our response? Does he decide who gets saved? Does he make us saved? Does he force us to go on being saved? In other words, is it his decision from beginning to end? Or is it dependent on my co-operation with his grace? That is the real question. I have no time for Pelagius and his idea that we can save ourselves – that is a gross distortion. But I have a lot of time for the French bishops.

Let us go back to the origins of these different views. I have told you that Augustine began his bishopric in North Africa believing in that middle picture I gave you: of co-operation with the grace of God, of seizing it by faith. That is where faith comes in; faith is getting hold of that lifebelt. It is not just by grace you are saved, it is by grace you are saved through *faith*. Faith is your part in this and your response to the offer. Augustine began thinking that way very well, but halfway through his ministry, he tried to combine Christian faith with what we call Greek Platonism. That suggests a very different kind of God, who is outside time, doesn't come and help us in time but just decides who gets saved; and from then on, I see a deterioration of Augustine's thinking. Many people think he had improved in his thinking. I believe he had gone the wrong way in it.

So in reaction to Pelagius, and his emphasis on the human will doing it all, he reacted to the other end and said: no, it is God's will only that does the saving; our wills are not involved at all. But the French bishops, who lived between

Italy and England and North Africa, took that middle view and said it is co-operation between freely offered grace and our faith. Unfortunately, Augustine very cleverly called them semi-Pelagians, which was rather naughty because it identified them with the other side. I think they were semi-Augustinians. They were right in the middle between the two. It was a naughty thing to give them Pelagius's name, but those French bishops knew where they were, and frankly that is where I would stand with them – right between North Africa and the British.

The British love to believe that it is our will that saves us. The favourite understanding of the British people about Christianity is *doing good*, isn't it? "I can be as good a Christian without going to church as any who go to church," they say. They have said it to me. It really is *do-it-yourself salvation*. Be kind to grandmother and the cat and you will finish up in heaven. That is typical do-gooding understanding of Christianity, and it is not the gospel. The gospel is: you will never be good enough. Only those who have tried to be good enough find that out. Wesley tried very hard to be good enough, Augustine did actually in his youth, and he found he couldn't make it. He found that it was grace that was needed to help him. If you try to be good enough, then you are measuring yourself by the wrong standard.

Years ago, I was having my hair cut by someone called Chris. I always went to his little shop to get my hair cut and to "get a load off my mind'. One day he was cutting my hair and he got part way around, and he suddenly said to me, "I'm as good as anyone who goes to your church."

I replied, "You may be. You would have to know them all, and know them all very well, to be able to say that, but nevertheless, that doesn't wash with me."

"Why not?"

"Well," I said, "Chris, are you as good as Jesus was?"

He said, "Yes." Now the conversation ended at that point because according to all my books on personal counselling, that shouldn't be the answer! So I was silent, and he worked his way further round my head, and said, "Well, perhaps not quite."

After that, he was climbing down all the way. You see, if you measure yourself by other people, you are good enough, and you are better than many. The trouble is that is pride, and the other side of pride is contempt, and the more you think yourself better than others, the more you think they are worse than you are. You are using the wrong measuring standard.

When you stand alongside Christ, your reaction will be Simon Peter's – "Depart from me for I'm a sinful man, O Lord." Jesus is the only person ever good enough to go into that new world that Father is going to make, but the glory of it is that he came to make it possible for us to be in that new world – *provided* we are willing to be made different people. That is the big proviso. It begins when you are justified by faith and you are restored to a relationship with God – without that, you never would be perfect because you would never make it on your own. But that is only restoring a relationship within which you can be made all that God wanted you to be. That is the good news – the gospel.

I have tried to give you those three pictures because that is where the real division of opinion lies, even in churches. There are people in church who think that the idea of being a Christian is to do your best and ask forgiveness for the rest, and that you will always be a mixture of good and bad. Therefore, you are told to come every Sunday and make confession because nobody expects you to be perfect. But if I go to an Anglican church, I don't say the confession because it says: "Ye that do truly and earnestly repent you of your sins..." and repentance means not doing them again. Repentance is always specific, not a blank cheque to cover anything you might have done the previous week. Confession is always confessing sins – plural. It is saying: I have done that this week and I repent of it and it is not going to happen next week. If people really mean the general confession prayer, it means that after fifty-two Sunday mornings, they have dealt with fifty-two separate sins which are now behind them and finished with. I just do not believe it is that easy. We should confess our sins – specific – and repent of them. A schoolboy once said: "Repentance is being sorry enough to stop" and that is a good definition. It means turning from sin to God, and you will find the grace of God enables you to do just that. If you really mean business, and if you are really confessing a specific sin, he will give you the grace to put it behind you, and you will hear Jesus' words to the woman taken in adultery: "Neither do I condemn you but don't do it again. Go and sin no more." I don't know what he would have said to her if she had been brought back six months later, having done it all over again. We don't know. We are not to exploit God's mercy or take advantage of it.

So I have tried to give you a picture of *saving grace*, and it is a gift of God. We could never make ourselves what he needs us to be in that new world. But he can do it. He is able to present us faultless before his throne of glory with exceeding joy. It does not say he is certain to, but it does say he is able to, and that is the good news. But it means that we need to be willing. Our wills are involved. When we are willing to be saved, we can be. When we are willing to be justified by faith, we can be. When we are willing to be sanctified, we can be – which does mean, as one preacher put it, every one of us is as holy as we really want to be. That is a devastating statement.

If he is *able* to make us holy, he does not want us to go on confessing sins, he wants us to be rid of them, and he can do it – if we are willing. But St Augustine (as he later became called) used to pray: "Lord, make me holy, but not just yet." That is a very human prayer. It is one of the most common mistakes about Christian preaching that what God wants is for us to be happy in this life and holy in the next. Actually, it is exactly the other way round – he wants us to be holy in this world and happy in the next. That is the gospel, and that is his offer. He is not just offering forgiveness for the past; he is offering holiness for the future. That will depend on whether we are willing, whether we trust and obey – that is faith, *continuing faith*, not just faith for one moment but faith for a lifetime, to go on trusting and obeying right to the end. Many would testify that it is toward the end that it can get more difficult to go on trusting and obeying. But have you noticed that Jesus said that it is he who is faithful to the end who gets saved – and he meant just that. We can't get round it.

At this point in our study there are two of my books that I want to recommend to you. The one that will be most relevant is *Once Saved, Always Saved?* and the other is *The Normal Christian Birth*, which explains how to get really started in the Christian life.

2

I have already mentioned the two wrong understandings of grace but now I want to expand on that. We shall first deal with *sovereign grace* and, secondly, with *free grace*. Let me first of all remind you of my definition of grace. I believe it is an *undeserved favour of God*. That definition covers every text in the New Testament. The second false view of grace is that it is an *irresistible force* – not an undeserved favour but an irresistible force that you cannot resist, and if God sets his grace on you, that is it. You cannot refuse it; you cannot resist it. It will make you get saved, it will keep you saved and ultimately will complete the job for you.

Now this view has a long history and I have mentioned already a bishop in North Africa that people call St Augustine, though I can never call him that. I believe that he, in his later years, did more damage to the Christian church than anybody else. Fortunately, the Eastern Orthodox churches were beyond his influence, but the Western churches, both Protestant and Catholic, have been profoundly affected by him. His basic misunderstanding was that God uses force, and that I believe is the fundamental error. He got it out of a parable of Jesus, where Jesus said a king held a great feast and sent invitations out and people made excuses and said no, sorry, can't come – I've bought a business, married a wife, whatever. So the king said: go out into the country lanes, don't just go into the streets of the town, go further afield and compel people to come in. My house shall be full, he said. Now that word *compel* Augustine fastened on. Ah – he says that we are to use force to get people into the kingdom. He took the word *compel* as meaning *force* – not persuade, but force. It was the result of his belief that God uses force on people that led to the later terrible abuses of the Crusades in which Christians felt they should use force to recapture the Holy Land for pilgrimage, and it led to the Inquisition where Jews were tortured until they were baptised. It was all justified on this use of the word compel, and if God compels people, then we are entitled to compel people. In other words, any method is acceptable to make somebody a Christian.

Well now, that was the basic mistake he made and it had profound repercussions over the next thousand years on the Christian church, and many of the things of which we are now ashamed were the result of saying that force is legitimate. I believe that God is omnipotent, that he is Almighty God and not – as one of my friends called him – "all-matey God". I believe he is Almighty, but I believe he does not use his force on people. He has created us to be voluntarily related to him. He does not want forced men and women in his kingdom because they won't be his sons and daughters. They won't have chosen it. He wants a family of people who have chosen to be saved and therefore responded to his love and grace. That is my own belief.

But from Augustine came most of the Protestant Reformation. Martin Luther was an Augustinian monk and therefore had been taught Augustine's teaching. John Calvin in Geneva had also imbibed Augustine's teaching, and his big two-volume work called *Institutes of the Christian Religion*, which is the teaching of Calvin, is nothing more than systematic Augustinianism.

So the major Protestant Reformers accepted Augustine's

teaching, and most of those in this country who call themselves *Reformed* theologians or Reformed Christians have picked up Augustine's teaching. It has become part of a whole systematic theology. Calvin himself was not responsible for what we call Calvinism today. Calvin did not believe it all, but I am afraid the five points of Calvinism, as they are called, came from Holland, from Calvin's successor in Geneva called Theodore Beza.

Those five points of Calvinism I want to go through with you now, because if they are true, then what I am telling you is untrue; and if what I am saying is true, then the five points of Calvinism are untrue. They come because of a man in Holland called Jacob Hermanszoon. I am sorry to quote all these names at you but you need to remember that these views have a long history, and Jacob Hermanszoon is one of my heroes. When he became a student, he adopted the habit of students adopting a Latin nickname, and he took the name *Arminius* which was the name of an ancient German warrior who defeated the Romans and kept them out of Germany. He thought it was a good name and he has been known ever since as Arminius. He was the royal chaplain. He preached every Sunday to the royal family in the biggest church in Amsterdam which is there today, just off the square which is called The Dam. He was such a godly, holy man that no-one dared criticise him while he was alive. As soon as he died, they called a conference (Synod) at a place called Dort. The Synod of Dort condemned Jacob Hermanszoon as a heretic, and produced the five points which we now call Calvinism. But they are Dutch, and the five points neatly fit into the word TULIP. Holland is noted for tulips, and this was one of the ugliest tulips that ever came out of Holland. But these were the five points which today are called Calvinism, and each of them depends on the other four. It is a whole system, and if you don't believe any one of them, the others will collapse too.

1. **T**otal Depravity
By that they mean we are absolutely helpless to do anything to respond to God. It leads to the extraordinary teaching that you have to be born again before you can even repent or believe, so that the new birth doesn't come after you repent and believe but before. And it is God's total sovereign will that decides who will be born again. So he picks people out to be born again, they are incapable of co-operating with the gospel, and the word *dead* comes in – they are so dead in trespasses and sins they cannot do anything at all. They are like drowned men in the sea. That is the first point of the five.

2. Unconditional Election
Put simply, that means that God chooses who is to be saved regardless of anything in them, even of his future knowledge of them. It is not anything to do with them. He decides. His election, his choice, of who is saved is totally unconditional. It is not in any way affected by the person being chosen, either what they are now or what they will be later. And God knows that, but he is not basing it on anything at all. If you ask why he saves some and not others, that is his *inscrutable will*. He has not told us and we are not to know. He is keeping that a secret.

3. Limited Atonement
Which means that Christ didn't die for the sins of the whole world. He only died for the sins of the chosen, the elect, the ones he would save, on the ground that: how could God punish sin twice? And if he punished Jesus for the sins of the whole world, how could he ever punish anyone again? That is the argument, and therefore they believe (which Calvin himself didn't believe incidentally) that Christ only died for some people and not for everybody.

4. Irresistible Grace
That once God has decided to save you, there is nothing you can do about that – you cannot refuse it, you cannot resist it because it is his will that matters, not yours, and therefore it is entirely within his sovereign will who he saves.

5. Perseverance of the Saints
I believe this is wrongly named. What it should be is *preservation* of the saints – that the same God who forced you to begin the Christian life will make sure that you end it, and that what he has begun he will decide to finish.

Now those five points form what we call "Calvinism" today, though I have told you that Calvin himself did not believe all five. He did not believe Limited Atonement – he believed that Jesus died for everybody. He did not believe in the Perseverance of the Saints. He believed you could fall from grace. But those five are the five points of this sovereign grace.

Now what are we to say about all this? It is the view that the two swimmers are drowned and can do nothing about it. They are dead. The lifeguard fishes one of them out but not the other, and pumps life into the first – and that is the picture of salvation I get from these five points. In other words, salvation does not depend on us – from beginning to end. It is his work and his alone. Our co-operation is not necessary. He is God. I will hand it to them that they have got a magnified view of the Lord. They have lifted the Lord so high in their estimation, that they have ruled out any autonomy of human nature. They have, I think, got too high a view of God: a God who settles everything up there; who decrees things in heaven that we can do nothing about here. That is a picture of God that I don't find in my

Bible. In the Bible I find a God who has decided to use his sovereignty to give us the freedom to say no to him; that he has chosen in his wisdom to make us able to resist him, to say no to him – right to the point of finishing up in hell. But he is a God who co-operates with people. We become his fellow workers. And I have in my Bible a picture of God who actually changes his mind in response to our prayer. Isn't that an amazing thought?

Moses prayed, and persuaded God not to wipe out the people of Israel. It says God repented and changed his mind. Amos does the same. These men knew that prayer works because God listens, and he is willing to change his plans in response to human prayer. Furthermore, in my Bible, God expresses regret; disappointment. Now if he knows everything that people are going to do in advance, how could he ever be disappointed? In Genesis 6 is the saddest verse in the Bible. It says that God regretted that he had made man. Well, if he knew everything beforehand, how could he regret it? It doesn't make sense. In other words, God is in a dynamic relationship with us by his choice. He is sovereign. And he will end history in the way he decides, make no mistake. Our freedom is only relative but it is there, and he made us capable of disobedience, and capable of rebellion. That was a big gamble but God took it.

In Noah's day he said that he regretted that he made man and that is totally different from the Greek Platonic view of God who never changes, never has feelings of regret or disappointment, who sits up in heaven way above all this kind of thing. The Bible does not hesitate to talk about God as if he were human – because we are made in his image and therefore we are like him. That is why – even though God does not have a physical body, he is Spirit – nevertheless we can talk about the hand of God, the fingers of God, the arm of God, the face of God, the ear of God, the mouth of God, and even the bowels of God and the feet of God. Now the Bible talks about this because God is real, and these physical attributes of ours correspond to something in God. God can walk, God can see, God can hear. He does not need ears to do that, but he can hear. It is this human side of God that Calvinism seems to ignore. It lifts him up beyond all this and somehow, he makes all his decisions up there without any regard for us, and without any response from us. That means we are just puppets. It means we are not human beings made in the image of God. It means we do not have the freedom to sin and the freedom to say no, the freedom to grieve his Holy Spirit, to resist his Spirit. We have the freedom to do all that because we are made in the image of God – and he, in his wisdom, and in power, took that risk. That is the Bible God and it is totally different from the idea of God who is outside of time. Time is real to my God. The Greek understanding of God was outside time. I don't know how many preachers I have heard preach that God is outside time and that one day in heaven we will be. Have you heard that said? It is so common but it does not come out of your Bible. In the Bible, God is in time – or, rather, time is in God. He is the God who was, and who is and who is to come; God to whom past, present and future matter.

Let me ask you a question just to prove this. Do you think God can change the past? I don't. I believe the past is as fixed for God as it is for us. He can change the present and the future, but God himself has no power to change the past. Thank him for that. Nobody can ever undo the cross now. It is done; it is fixed. It is a historical fact and nobody can change it – not even God himself. Time matters to God.

You know, when I was a student at Cambridge, I nearly lost my faith because the tutors taught me to read the Bible with a pair of scissors and to cut this out and to cut that out, and after two years of that, I could not preach. What saved my faith were two books, one of them entitled *Christ and Time* by a Swiss theologian. That man restored my faith in a God who is in time, a God to whom past, present and future matter, who is working out his whole programme through history. I realised that history is his story. Once you realise that, the whole Bible opens up in a new way because it is full of history and it is all his story. It is the story of what God has done inside time and space. I believe he is greater than time and space, but he is the God who works *in* time and space – that is the message of the whole Bible. He works with human beings. He can overrule, but he gives us the freedom not to co-operate. Thank you, Lord, for honouring us in that way.

But what an embarrassment it is to us that so many people will not co-operate with God. There is only one end to that; it is a serious end. God will *throw* them into hell. You know, it never says in the Bible that God sends people to hell. It always says he throws them there. Why? Because they have become rubbish. What do you do with something that has become useless to you? You throw it in the bin. You don't place it there; you throw it there. It is no longer any use. That is what *perishing* means. If you have got a hot water bottle and it has perished, no use to you, you throw it away. The tragedy is that there will be millions of people whom God throws away. That is why we want to get them saved. That is the opposite to being saved – to become utterly useless to God.

The system of five points of Calvinism I believe has too high a view of God and too low a view of humans, and a wrong view of the relationship between the two. The whole Bible is about God seeking our co-operation, the response of our wills to his will. He wills that all men should be saved, but that depends on the response of our will to be one of the saved. So that is sovereign grace, and the biggest question it raises for me is why some people are saved and not others. Under sovereign grace, the answer is entirely in his hands, nothing to do with us, and as I say, it is no better than being in a heavenly lottery. It raises a big question with me: why bother to preach the gospel? If I believed that only the people who have been elected by God will respond to what I say and that those who are not chosen by God *cannot respond*, I would feel that I would be wasting my time. I would not be constrained to be preaching the gospel if that were what I believed. But – and here I declare something you could take wrongly, but I mean it – most of my Calvinist friends keep it in the study, and when they get into the pulpit, they are good Arminians. I am so thankful for that.

Charles Haddon Spurgeon was a noted Calvinist but he used to pray before every service: "Lord, save all the elect and then elect some more." And he preached as if anybody could respond to the gospel. When Calvinist friends of mine keep it in the study and don't take it into the pulpit, they preach as if God loves everybody and wants everybody to be saved. Hallelujah for that. It is not easy to preach Calvinism. You are really telling people that if your number is not in God's hand, your number's up.

In other words, Jesus said go and preach the gospel to every creature – everybody deserves to hear the good news, and it is up to *them* whether they respond or not. It is not up to God, it is up to them. God's grace is offered to all but not all will accept it. That is where I stand, and I believe that it is not only the biblical stand, I believe it is the common sense stand. Your common sense tells you that is the real situation, and that the reason why people are not being saved is their own choice. If it is not their own choice, there cannot be a Day of Judgment. God could not possibly decide who deserves to be lost and who deserves to be saved on the basis of: it's only his decision.

I think I have said enough about that; except when I talk about *free grace*, though it is very different, there is one thing in common between sovereign grace and free grace. They both believe 'once saved, always saved' – meaning that once you have started the Christian life, that is it – you are safe. And I find that people don't want to be saved from their sins, they want to be safe from hell. That is a very different business. God wants us to be *saved* – not to be safe, but to be saved. The question is: can the process of salvation be stopped? Can it be slowed up? Can it even be sent backwards? We shall look at that soon.

But first I want to talk about *free grace*. Now let us make it quite clear: you cannot buy the grace of God. You can't earn it. You can't deserve it. You can't merit it. So doesn't that mean it is free? From one point of view, yes; but if you mean that it is free because you don't need to do anything yourself, then the answer is no.

Unfortunately, many people have misunderstood the word *works*. Now "by grace are you saved, not of works." But that does not mean that you don't have to *do* anything to be saved. Go back to the throwing the lifebelt into the sea. You are saying: get hold of this and I will pull you safe to the shore. But getting hold of the lifebelt is something the drowning man has to do. That is not *works*! The word *works* when Paul uses it means *good deeds* – that you have got to have good deeds to be saved, and that is not the truth. But that is different from saying you don't need to do anything. That is what a teaching called *free grace* is now spreading around the world. It is coming from a very prominent preacher in Singapore at the moment, and on the Internet it is spreading everywhere. I found it everywhere in South Africa – from Singapore – when I went. So what are they teaching? They are teaching: you are saved without doing anything, very similar to sovereign grace, but it is a different view.

To bring it right home to you perhaps, I will tell you two things they teach based on that. First of all, they say repentance is not necessary for salvation or forgiveness, because repentance is something you do. So they teach that in gospel preaching we should never call on people to repent of their sins because that is telling them to do something. They say the only thing that God wants from you is faith and that is not something you do. Isn't it? The word *works* does not always mean good deeds. It can simply mean *action*, and James 2 says: "Faith without action is dead." It cannot save. It is not saying faith without good deeds, it is saying: faith without acting on it. He is saying that *professing* faith does not save, but *practising* faith does save.

We had three children. One is now in heaven, the other two are still on earth, and we played a game called "Faith" when they were little. We would go to the staircase and they would climb up four or five steps and stand, three of them in a row, and then they would say, "Daddy, if we jump, will you catch us?" I used to say, "I might and I might not," and I kept my hands behind my back. I said, "The only way you'll find out is if you jump." They loved this game. It was their equivalent of video nasties before video nasties came. They would stand on the steps and their little tummies would turn over, and then one of them would jump and I would catch them. That encouraged the other two to try it and they would jump and I would catch them. We don't play the game now – for health and safety reasons – *my* safety, because they are adults now! But that is how I taught them that faith is jumping, it is acting, it is doing something about it. It is not saying "I believe"; it is proving that you believe by taking a step, and taking a risk that you will fall flat on your face if the Lord is not there to catch you. That is *actions of faith – faith works*. Not good works but faith works. James gives you two examples – of a bad woman who figured in our Lord's genealogy, a prostitute, and a good man called Abraham – and they both took great risks for their future. James says that is what faith is – when you act on it, when you do something that you will fall flat on your face if the Lord doesn't catch you. There is an awful lot of professed faith around but there is not so much practised faith – but that is what practised faith is.

Let me give you a simple example. I was due to go to a Muslim country in the Far East and my passport had nearly twenty Israeli stamps in it. When I left the airport in a safe country, they looked at my passport in the emigration part and said, "You won't get in to the country where you're going to, Mr Pawson."

"Why not?"

"Well, you've got Israel on most of the pages of your passport."

I said, "They're expecting me; I'm going."

I landed in the Muslim country at the main airport and got to the immigration officer and he said, "Your passport please," and I handed it over.

I said, "Lord, blind him – just blind him." He took my passport and went through every page without looking at it. He went right through the whole passport gazing into the distance and then handed it back to me.

Thank you, Lord. It is just a little thing but I had to have the sort of faith that runs the risk.

When I smuggled Bibles into China, I had the same sort of experience. The trouble is life is so comfortable and easy for us most of the time, we don't have to live by faith. But real saving faith is faith with action. Faith is something you do; and repentance is something you do, and unless you repent, you can't be forgiven – not in my Bible. It even says – when Jesus said, forgive your brother seven times a day – "if he repents". Many people have never noticed that you know.

How can you forgive if someone doesn't repent? Well, you can see that you are not bitter – that is not forgiveness. Forgiveness is restoring a relationship with someone, and if they don't repent, how can you restore the relationship? It is impossible.

Are these new truths to you? I am bringing them home to you, I hope, in a sharper way because these are the truths of scripture. We are not playing games with God. He is a righteous God. We should remember that. Have you heard the phrase "the unconditional love of God"? You never found that phrase in your Bible. I find verses like "God loves those who fear him"; "God loves those who keep his commandments". Jesus said: if you love me, you will keep my commandments and my Father will love you. Is that unconditional love? No, it is a righteous love.

Let us look further at *free grace*. Two books are circulating. One is entitled *Absolutely Free* and the other is called *Free of Charge*. They are typical of the books that are going around the world at the moment and saying, (1) You don't need to repent to be forgiven; and (2) and this is very serious – when you are forgiven, God has forgiven all your future sins as well as your past. Have you ever heard such a thing? That means that if you are a Christian, it doesn't matter how you live. In South Africa I found this teaching had got such a hold on Christians that it no longer mattered if they lived a sinful life or a holy life because God has forgiven *all* my sins; all the sins I have not committed yet he has forgiven. I can't find that anywhere in my Bible. I find that Christians who sin can deal with it; that if we go on confessing our sins, he is faithful and righteous to go on forgiving our sins, and the blood of Jesus goes on cleansing us. It is a continuous thing. It is not: I came to Christ and all my sins are gone, though there are even hymns which say that – but your Bible doesn't. Your future sins matter to God terribly. In fact, I believe it is more serious when you are a Christian and sin than it was before, because now you know. Read a chapter like Hebrews 10 and you find that those who *know* what sin is are more guilty than those who don't; and that to go back into your old way of life after you have found the truth is to be worse off than if you had never known the way of salvation. (I am quoting Peter now.)

These are serious words in scripture. It does matter when a Christian sins. It matters more to the Lord. But it can be dealt with and there is a way you find in 1 John 1 for dealing with it, because we have an Advocate in heaven who will stand for our defence. We have an accuser in heaven, an accuser of the brethren, because Satan is not in hell, he is in heaven according to my Bible. He is going to be thrown out of heaven one day, hallelujah, but then he will come to earth and do his worst here. But at the moment Satan loves to accuse God's people of sin. He loves to say God, Did you see what one of your people has just done? He is doing it all the time. Fortunately, he doesn't get away with it because there is someone else who is pleading for us: "we have an Advocate" – Jesus himself – always praying for us. But these are serious matters. It is a serious thing when Christians sin, and they cannot just hold up a ticket to heaven and say, I am alright, I am still going there. It doesn't work that way.

So how did this free grace movement deal with all the texts in Scripture that tell us what we need to do? The free grace teaching is that you don't need to do anything, just believe – and by believe, they mean something inside you, they don't mean *acting on it*. They mean professing faith – that's all you need to do. Well, how do they deal with the New Testament? In a very subtle and simple way – they have divided all the teaching in the New Testament into two separate categories. They label one "Salvation" and the other "Discipleship". They split the two completely: one is to be saved and taken to heaven; the other is to become a disciple of Jesus – and everything we are told to do in the New Testament belongs to discipleship and not to salvation. I am trying to explain how they reach this extraordinary position of: you don't need to do anything. For discipleship, you need to do things, but that doesn't belong to your salvation. The most you can lose by not being a disciple is a reward in heaven, but you will still go there because heaven comes to your salvation, and there is nothing for you to do to be saved.

Where do they get this from? The answer is they are building it – and these two books do the same – on one verse in the book of Acts, and the whole of John's Gospel. The one verse in the book of Acts is where Paul said to the Philippian jailer (who had said, "What must I do to be saved?) "Believe on the Lord Jesus Christ and you will be saved." And they say that is all that is needed for salvation. But Paul clearly didn't stop there because before daylight dawned, he had baptised them all, so he had told them they must be baptised. In fact, my book *The Normal Christian Birth* is based on the belief that to begin to be saved you need to do four things. You need to *Repent* of your sin, *Believe* in the Lord Jesus, be *Baptised* in water and *Receive* the Holy Spirit. There are four things to do to appropriate grace and be saved, and that book spells all those out. I am happy to say that it is now being used in many Bible Schools for real basic teaching on how to be saved.

One verse in Acts is not enough because there are other verses in Acts that talk about repenting, other verses that talk about being baptised, and there are other verses that talk about receiving the Holy Spirit. Put them all together and there are clearly four things. It is interesting that, on the day of Pentecost, when Peter finished preaching, they said, what shall we *do*? The free grace people would say, "Nothing." Peter said, "Repent, and be baptised every one of you for the forgiveness of sins and you shall receive the gift of the Holy Spirit." He didn't even tell them to believe, because their very question told him they already believed what he had been saying, and he was telling them what they needed to *do*. But the free grace people say: no, only believe.

It is comparatively easy to profess belief. Do you know, I was in a very posh, modern church building in Germany and a well-dressed lady in the front row put her hand up when I said, "How many of you believe in me?" And I said to her: "You profess to believe in me but I don't know if you do or not. If you gave me your money to look after, that would be proof that you believe in me." The place went frozen, and afterwards the pastor said, "Do you realise who that was? She is the richest woman in this city." Her husband owned most of the property in the middle of the city and he died and left it all to her and she was fabulously wealthy. In fact, I got the impression that she had probably paid for the beautiful new church building, and I had said to her: "Give me your money and I'll know you believe in me."

Seriously, I don't know if you believe in me. You would have to do something to show me that you trusted or obeyed me. When you trust someone, you obey them. You do what they tell you. If you would get into my car with me, I would know that you trust me – at least as far as my driving is concerned. I would say, "Come on, get in," and your getting in would show me you trusted me as a driver. There are two people in this world whose cars I will never get in again. I do not trust them, and one of them I had to remind to drive on the left hand side of the road! We were just chasing round corners on the right hand side, and his wife was having hysterics, and I would never get in the car again. If you trust someone you will do what they tell you – it is as simple as that. If you trust Jesus, you will obey him. And when you disobey him, you will feel dreadful. You will know it, and you can deal with that. That is the difference between being a Christian and not being one.

But they say that the whole of John's Gospel tells us that we don't need to repent, for the simple reason that that Gospel never uses the word repent – not even when Jesus talked to Nicodemus. It is true that it doesn't. Ah! But there is an answer to that. John's Gospel was not written for unbelievers. He says at the end of the Gospel that if everything that Jesus said were written down, the world could not contain the books. But he said: these are written that you may go on believing that Jesus is the Son of God and, going on believing, you will go on having life in his name. You notice that I have been adding some English words in there – *going on*. Because – you will have to take my word for it, or check up – present continuous tense in the Greek means to go on doing something, and every time the word *believe* comes in John's Gospel, it says *go on believing*.

John 3:16 is a case in point. "For God so loved the world that he gave his only begotten Son that whoever *goes on believing* in him will never perish but *go on having* eternal life." When you became a Christian, God didn't pack a thing called "life" and give it to you, because life isn't a thing. Life is people, again like grace. And your eternal life you only have *in Christ*. You don't have it in you. That is why Jesus said: stay in me; abide in me; reside in me; stay in me – because if a branch does not stay in the vine it will die. It will become fruitless and dead and it will have to be cut off, pruned. That is one of those amazing teachings of Jesus which is against "once saved always saved". Jesus said: stay in me and you will bear much fruit; but if you don't stay in me, the branch withers and dies, becomes fruitless *and is cut off and burned*. Stay in Christ. You only have life in Christ, as John puts it somewhere else – he said, this life is in his Son and those who stay in him have life – and those who don't, lose it. You don't have eternal life in you, you have it in him – in Christ; and outside of Christ, you lose life. The life is in the vine, not in the branches; and the branches draw the life from the vine.

So John's Gospel never does say repent, and these free grace people say: well, if John was written to help people to believe, we don't need to repent. No, it was written to help people to go on believing; it is written for people who have been Christians some years. That is why it doesn't mention baptism and it doesn't mention repentance – because these things belong to the beginning of the Christian life. He is wanting them to go on believing, and every time the word "believe" is in John's Gospel, it is in the present continuous tense – to go on believing.

This brings me to the final question: once saved, always saved? I believe that is not the truth and I am afraid it has led many Christians into a complacency, a false assurance, that has made them indifferent. "It's alright, I'm going to heaven." A man on a train going up to Waterloo told me to my face: "I've left my wife and I'm now living with another woman. I am a Christian. I heard you preach years ago. If I marry this woman and divorce my wife, will that put it right in God's sight?"

I said, "No. You've got a choice. You either go back to your wife now and live with her and you can live with Christ in the new world. Or you can live with this woman and not with Christ in the next world."

Was that a harsh thing to say? I only had two minutes. He only got on at Clapham Junction and he ran away from me at Waterloo. But I wanted to say something that he couldn't get out of his mind – that he had a choice, and that he must do the right thing in the Lord's sight.

I have written on that very subject, divorce and remarriage, *Remarriage after Divorce is Adultery Unless...* because it is one of the lies that has been almost accepted in the church, that remarriage after divorce is acceptable to God. Churches are saying this all over the place and there are now as many broken marriages in church as there are outside as a result. But I found this exact thing in South Africa. The pastors were complaining to me. They said: divorces and remarriages are happening in our congregation; we don't seem able to stop it. But it is because they did not teach that we need to go on trusting and obeying the Lord, not just once but for a lifetime, and to endure to the end and be saved. My book is available if you are concerned – as I am – about that very subject. So why, biblically, do I believe that "once saved, always saved" is misleading? First because in the Bible, the texts are always balanced. If there is a text at the end of Jude that says "he is able to present us faultless before his throne of glory", just a few verses ahead of that, "keep yourselves in the love of God". He is able to keep, but keep yourselves. There is a balance there. Similarly, in Paul's letters to Timothy and Titus, he says: "He is able to keep what I have committed to him against that day". That is true, and it is a popular chorus too. But just turn the page and what Paul says is this: "I have kept the faith". You see the balance there? He is able to keep, but we need to do our part in the keeping. It is co-operation again. He calls us to be his, and we call on him to be saved – his call; our call.

All the way through the New Testament you can choose verses out of context that suggest it is all his doing and you can choose other verses that say it is our doing. The answer is: it is both! He calls us, we call on him – that is how we get saved. He is able to keep us; we keep ourselves in his love.

Jesus spoke on hell more than anyone else in the Bible. That is why I believe in it. In fact, other people in the Bible did not talk about hell but Jesus did. But out of all his many warnings, only two were for the Pharisees, and all the rest were for his own followers. Did you ever notice that? Jesus warned his disciples about hell frequently, and I fear ending up there because Jesus warned his own born-again believing followers that they could end up there. So did Paul. He feared it himself, lest having preached to others, he be disqualified himself. There are passages in Revelation, the last book in the Bible, which clearly state that the new world – the new heaven and the new earth – are not for all believers but for *overcomers*: he who *overcomes* shall inherit all this. What does he mean? He also says, on the negative side, that those who overcome will not have their names blotted out from the Book of Life. That, surely, is the most terrible thing that could happen to a human being – once having got their name in that book, to have it rubbed out. The Book of Life is mentioned four times in the Bible, and three of those times talk about having names blotted out. So Revelation tells us that overcomers will get into the new universe – those who overcome temptation inside and persecution outside are those who will be fit for the new world. Check me out.

There are eighty passages in the New Testament warning believers not to lose what they have found in Christ. I have referred to some of them already, but read Romans 11 right through. Paul says to Gentile believers many of the Jews were cut off because they stopped believing, and then he says: do you think God will deal differently with you? And he tells them: continue in his love; that, unless you continue in his love, you too will be cut off. Amazing! I have never heard a preacher quote that verse, but it is there in your Bible. I refer to those eighty passages in my book *Once Saved Always Saved?* if you want to look them up. Eighty passages in the Word of God cannot be wrong. It is overwhelming. It is the sovereign grace and the free grace movements that teach that once you have started on the way of salvation, you finish on it automatically, inevitably, because of God. But my Bible doesn't say that. It says: make every effort after that holiness without which no man will see the Lord. That is serious. It means, we are not *saved* yet, and we need to press on like Paul, forgetting the things that are behind, and looking forward to the things that are ahead, let us press on – let us keep going, let us keep continuing to trust and obey the Lord Jesus, and we will be saved.

We looked at *saving grace* and what that really means. We have looked at *sovereign grace* which puts it all in God's court. We have looked at *free grace* which says that discipleship and salvation are two different things. To me, salvation is following Jesus – it is discipleship. It is the same thing, and it all hangs together. And we are to be disciples of Jesus – that is the most common word for Christians in the New Testament. Not believers, not Christians – that was a nickname – but *disciples*, and a disciple is someone who goes on learning, and who goes on following and who clings as close to the Master as he can. And that is what I believe we are called to do.

ABOUT DAVID PAWSON

A speaker and author with uncompromising faithfulness to the Holy Scriptures, David brings clarity and a message of urgency to Christians to uncover hidden treasures in God's Word.

Born in England in 1930, David began his career with a degree in Agriculture from Durham University. When God intervened and called him to become a Minister, he completed an MA in Theology at Cambridge University and served as a Chaplain in the Royal Air Force for three years. He moved on to pastor several churches, including the Millmead Centre in Guildford, which became a model for many UK church leaders. In 1979, the Lord led him into an international ministry. His current itinerant ministry is predominantly to church leaders. David and his wife Enid currently reside in the county of Hampshire in the UK.

Over the years, he has written a large number of books, booklets, and daily reading notes. His extensive and very accessible overviews of the books of the Bible have been published and recorded in *Unlocking the Bible*. Millions of copies of his teachings have been distributed in more than 120 countries, providing a solid biblical foundation.

He is reputed to be the "most influential Western preacher in China" through the broadcast of his best-selling *Unlocking the Bible* series into every Chinese province by Good TV. In the UK, David's teachings are often broadcast on Revelation TV.

Countless believers worldwide have also benefited from his generous decision in 2011 to make available his extensive audio video teaching library free of charge at www.davidpawson.org and we have recently uploaded all of David's video to a dedicated channel on www.youtube.com

TAKE A LOOK AT YOUTUBE
www.youtube.com/user/DavidPawsonMinistry

THE EXPLAINING SERIES
BIBLICAL TRUTHS SIMPLY EXPLAINED

If you have been blessed reading this book, there are more available in the series. Please register to download more booklets for free by visiting
www.explainingbiblicaltruth.global

Other booklets in the *Explaining* series will include:
The Amazing Story of Jesus
The Resurrection: *The Heart of Christianity*
Studying the Bible
Being Anointed and Filled with the Holy Spirit
New Testament Baptism
How to study a book of the Bible: Jude
The Key Steps to Becoming a Christian
What the Bible says about Money
What the Bible says about Work
Grace – *Undeserved Favour, Irresistible Force or Unconditional Forgiveness?*
Eternally secure? – *What the Bible says about being saved*
De-Greecing the Church – The impact of Greek thinking on Christian beliefs
Three texts often taken out of context: *Expounding the truth and exposing error*
The Trinity
The Truth about Christmas

They will also be available to purchase as print copies from:
Amazon or **www.thebookdepository.com**

UNLOCKING THE BIBLE

A unique overview of both the Old and New Testaments, from internationally acclaimed evangelical speaker and author David Pawson. *Unlocking the Bible* opens up the Word of God in a fresh and powerful way. Avoiding the small detail of verse by verse studies, it sets out the epic story of God and his people in Israel. The culture, historical background and people are introduced and the teaching applied to the modern world. Eight volumes have been brought into one compact and easy to use guide to cover both the Old and New Testaments in one massive omnibus edition. *The Old Testament: The Maker's Instructions* (The five books of law); *A Land and A Kingdom* (Joshua, Judges, Ruth, 1&2 Samuel, 1&2 Kings); *Poems of Worship and Wisdom* (Psalms, Song of Solomon, Proverbs, Ecclesiastes, Job); *Decline and Fall of an Empire* (Isaiah, Jeremiah and other prophets); *The Struggle to Survive* (Chronicles and prophets of exile); *The New Testament: The Hinge of History* (Mathew, Mark, Luke, John and Acts); *The Thirteenth Apostle* (Paul and his letters); *Through Suffering to Glory* (Hebrews, the letters of James, Peter and Jude, the Book of Revelation). Already an international bestseller.

JESUS: THE SEVEN WONDERS OF HISTORY

This book is the result of a lifetime of telling 'the greatest story ever told' around the world. David re-told it to many hundreds of young people in Kansas City, USA, who heard it with uninhibited enthusiasm, 'tweeting' on the internet about 'this cute old English gentleman' even while he was speaking.

Taking the middle section of the Apostles' Creed as a framework, David explains the fundamental facts about Jesus on which the Christian faith is based in a fresh and stimulating way. Both old and new Christians will benefit from this 'back to basics' call and find themselves falling in love with their Lord all over again.

OTHER TEACHINGS
BY DAVID PAWSON

For the most up to date list of David's Books go to: **www.davidpawsonbooks.com**

To purchase David's Teachings go to: **www.davidpawson.com**

www.ingramcontent.com/pod-product-compliance
Lightning Source LLC
Chambersburg PA
CBHW071037080526
44587CB00015B/2661